British Library Cataloguing in Publication Data
available on request

ISBN 0-7112-0679-1 paperback

Printed in Hong Kong

5 7 9 8 6 4

Art Direction by Debbie MacKinnon
Design by Sarah Mackenzie

HOW GREEN ARE YOU?

by
DAVID BELLAMY
illustrated by Penny Dann

Contents

FRANCES LINCOLN

Meet the whales

Whales have lived on Earth for millions of years longer than we have. They live in the oceans, but they are not fish — they are mammals like us. Their babies feed on their mothers' milk.

Whales live in family groups. They talk to each other in high-pitched calls and the humpback whales sing beautiful songs. This page shows how whales live and what they need.

Dolphins

Whales need clean water and plenty of space. Some kinds of whale travel vast distances across the oceans from their feeding grounds to their breeding grounds.

Whales need food to eat. Some toothed whales feed on fish and squid, but killer whales may also eat penguins, seals and even other whales.

Killer whale

4

Do you know?

Blue whale 30 metres

If you and your friends lay end to end, it would take 23 of you to match the length of a blue whale.

Sperm whale 20 metres

Humpback whale 18 metres

Porpoise 2 metres

20,000 km
equator

Blue whales feed in the Arctic or Antarctic and swim nearly 20,000 km to warm tropical water to breed. The journey takes 3 months.

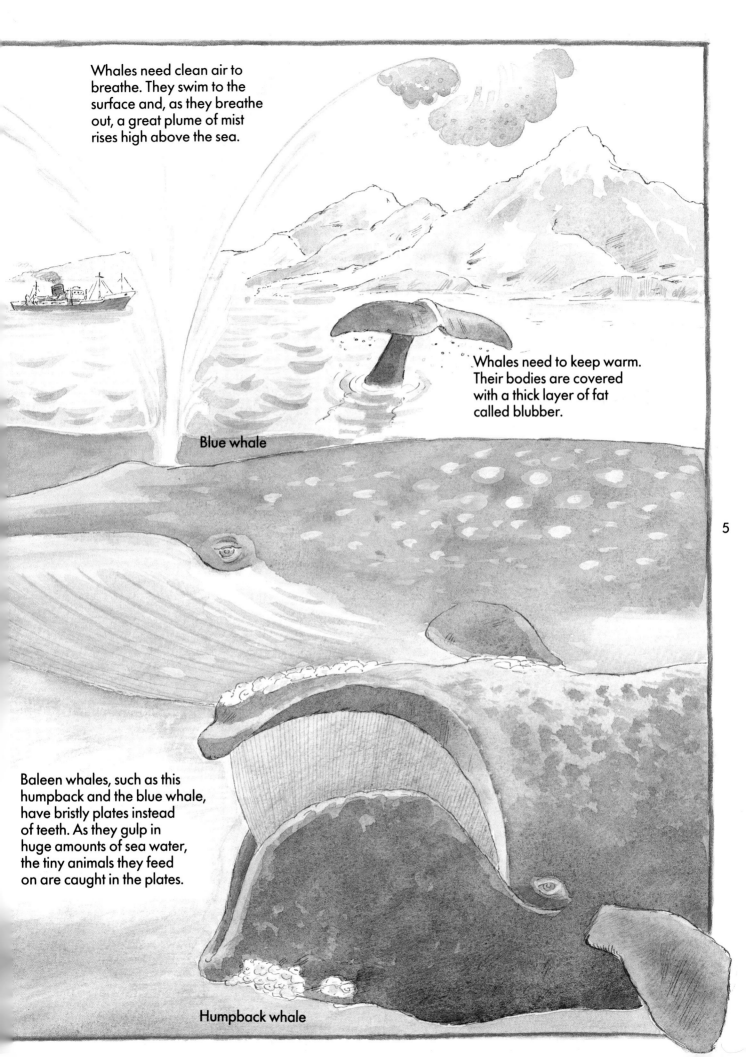

Whales need clean air to breathe. They swim to the surface and, as they breathe out, a great plume of mist rises high above the sea.

Whales need to keep warm. Their bodies are covered with a thick layer of fat called blubber.

Blue whale

Baleen whales, such as this humpback and the blue whale, have bristly plates instead of teeth. As they gulp in huge amounts of sea water, the tiny animals they feed on are caught in the plates.

Humpback whale

Meet the people

People, like whales, need air to breathe, food to eat, and a way of keeping warm. But there are now so many of us — over five billion — that we are damaging the Earth.

More and more land is used for farming, for roads and for homes. More and more factories use electricity, steel, wood and chemicals to make all kinds of things, from light bulbs to jumbo jets.

Farms cover much of the countryside. The cows in this field are eating grass. We shall drink their milk or it will be made into cheese, butter or yoghurt.

DANGER

These power stations are making electricity by burning coal and oil. Coal and oil are taken from the ground and one day there will be none left.

Factories make the things we use such as clothes, toys, cars and tractors. If they are not run properly, they can fill the air with dirty smoke and the rivers with dirty water.

These pylons are carrying electricity to houses, shops, offices and factories.

Cars carry people, and trucks carry goods from place to place. They help us, but they use fuel made from oil and make fumes which pollute the air. They are also noisy, and roads and car parks take up a lot of space.

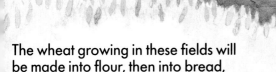

The wheat growing in these fields will be made into flour, then into bread, cakes, pasta and other food.

What is the environment?

The environment is all the things we need to be able to live – clean water to drink and to wash with, space to live and move about in, fresh air to breathe and food to eat. We could not live without plants and animals. They help to make the soil, they clean the water and the air, and they provide us with all our food.

What is pollution?

Animals, people, cars and factories all produce waste. This is not a problem if the amount of waste is small and it can break down to become a harmless part of the soil, sea or air. But when there is too much waste, or when the waste contains poisons, it pollutes the environment.

How the whale can help us

Only 400 years ago, there were many whales of all kinds. They had few enemies until people started hunting them. Then so many whales were killed that some kinds nearly became extinct.

In the last 20 years people have persuaded most governments round the world to stop the killing of whales — and now the number of whales is beginning to grow again.

The Friendly Whale says thank you for helping to save the whales. Now she is going to help us save ourselves. The letters **W**, **H**, **A**, **L** and **E** stand for **Water**, **Habitat**, **Air**, **Life** and **Energy** — the five most important parts of our environment. Each of these is in danger.

Water

We need clean water to drink, to cook with and to wash with. When we have finished with it, we throw it away. Every day lots of dirt and chemicals pour into the rivers and seas from our homes, factories and farms.
We use so much water that there is often not enough to go round.

The Friendly Whale says look for this symbol in the rest of the book to see how you can save water and make your waste water cleaner.

Habitat

The oceans are the habitat of the whales — the space in which they live. The world is our habitat. We use its resources. We chop down forests for wood, and build farms, houses, roads and factories on the land. We dig mines and quarries and let our waste pollute the ground, sea and air.

The Friendly Whale says look for this symbol to see how to save some of the Earth's resources and make less waste.

Air

We, like the whales, need clean air to breathe. But the air also protects us from the harmful rays of the sun and stops the Earth getting too hot or too cold.
Some of the chemicals we use in fridges and aerosols are damaging the air, and fumes from cars, power stations and factories are polluting it.

The Friendly Whale says look for this symbol to see how to make the air cleaner.

Life

We have helped to save the whales from extinction but every day more than 10 sorts of plants and animals become extinct.
By the year 2000 more than a million kinds of plants and animals may have been wiped out. Most of these plants and animals come from the huge rainforests that grow near the equator.

The Friendly Whale says look for this symbol and do what you can to help plants and animals.

Energy

Energy is what makes things work. The food you eat gives you energy to run and jump. Cars and trucks burn petrol or oil to make them go. Cookers, heaters and many other things use the energy of gas, or electricity, which is made by burning oil or coal. We get oil, coal and gas from deep under the ground, but soon there will be none left.

The Friendly Whale says look for this symbol to see how to save energy.

Please switch off after use.

In the bathroom

How much dirty water do you pour down the drains every day? It is not only the dirt but the soap and chemical cleaners too that spoil the water.

The Friendly Whale shows how you and your family can use less water and keep clean without harming the environment too much.

W. Save water! Ask your parents to put a brick in the cistern so that you won't flush so much water down the toilet each time.

L. Make sure your shampoos, hair conditioners, creams and lotions have not been tested on animals. Make especially sure they do not contain whale oil.

H. Make sure the cleaners for your bath, sink and toilet are biodegradable, to keep your waste water cleaner.

Help the environment by asking your parents to use biodegradable washing powder in the washing machine. They can save energy and water by making sure they have a full load of dirty clothes every time.

Save water by taking a shower instead of a bath. This saves energy too, because you'll use less hot water and won't use so much electricity, gas or oil.

Use less soap and shampoo. The bubbles are nice but wasteful.

BIODEGRADABLE

Do you know?

- We each use about 45,500 litres of water a year, enough to fill more than a tanker lorry.

- One third of all this water is flushed down the toilet.

15,000 litres

- Almost half of all the water which falls on the land as rain or snow is used by people.

What is biodegradable?

Trees are litter louts, dropping millions of leaves every autumn. But their litter is biodegradable. The leaves rot and slowly disappear into the soil, making it rich and healthy. Many chemical cleaners and plastics do not rot, because they are not biodegradable. Instead they stay in the soil or water and can poison it.

In the kitchen

You may not think that what you do inside your home can affect the air high in the sky, up to 20 kilometres above your head, but it does. When power stations burn oil or coal to make your electricity, tonnes of smoke pour from their chimneys and pollute the air. The Friendly Whale shows how you can help to save electricity and make the air cleaner.

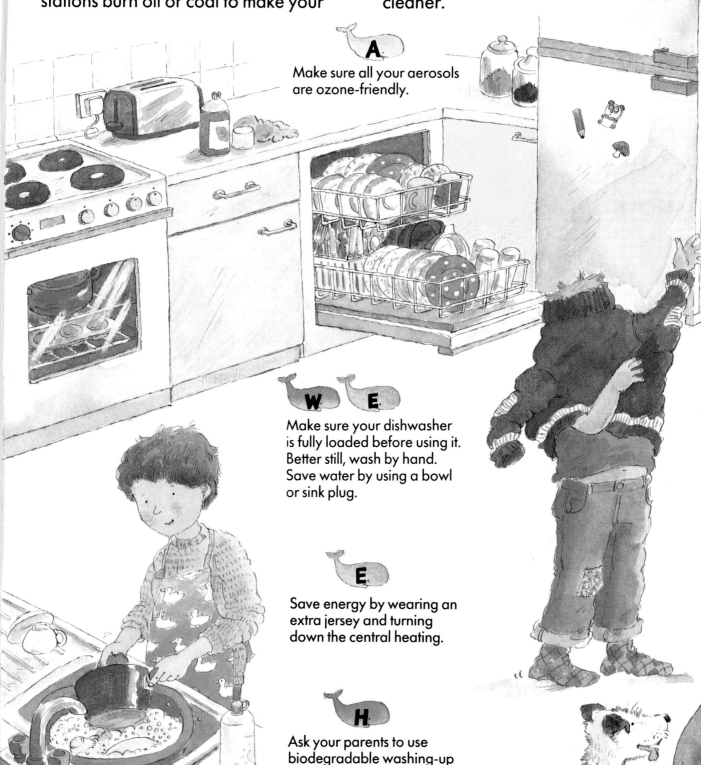

A Make sure all your aerosols are ozone-friendly.

W E Make sure your dishwasher is fully loaded before using it. Better still, wash by hand. Save water by using a bowl or sink plug.

E Save energy by wearing an extra jersey and turning down the central heating.

H Ask your parents to use biodegradable washing-up liquid.

W. Save water in dry weather by using washing-up water on your garden. Pour the water on the soil, not on the plants.

E **A.** Open the fridge door as little as possible. When warm air gets in, extra electricity is needed to cool it down again.

A. Make sure your take-away food is packed in ozone-friendly boxes. Ask before you buy!

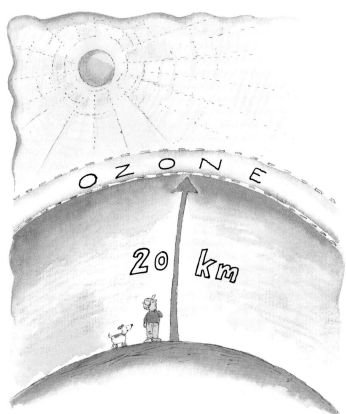

O Z O N E

20 km

What is ozone-friendly?

There is a layer of ozone gas 20 kilometres above the Earth. It stops most of the sun's harmful rays from reaching us. But recently the ozone layer has become much thinner in places and even has large holes in it.

We know that chemicals called CFCs, which we use in fridges, aerosols and some foam packing, can destroy ozone. Ozone-friendly aerosols and packing do not contain CFCs.

Do you know?

• Very soon new fridges will be made without harmful CFCs.

What's in the dustbin?

We throw away huge amounts of rubbish every day. People in poorer countries cannot afford to waste anything. They mend and use again whatever they can.
The Friendly Whale shows how we too can re-use or recycle much of the rubbish in our dustbins.

H E

Save aluminium and tin cans to be recycled. Use a magnet to tell them apart – tin cans stick, aluminium ones do not. If you re-use metals, you take less from the Earth.

H L

Find a shop which will re-use your empty egg-boxes.

H L

Save old newspapers to be recycled. Paper is made from trees, so when you save it you save trees and forests too.
Pass old magazines and comics on to someone else, perhaps to a hospital or to your doctor or dentist for their waiting rooms.

H L

Pass on old clothes and toys to someone else, either to younger friends or a jumble sale. Very old cotton and woollen clothes can be used as rags, then either recycled, or shredded and put on the compost heap.

H E

Wash and keep plastic containers. They can be used as storage boxes or as plant pots.

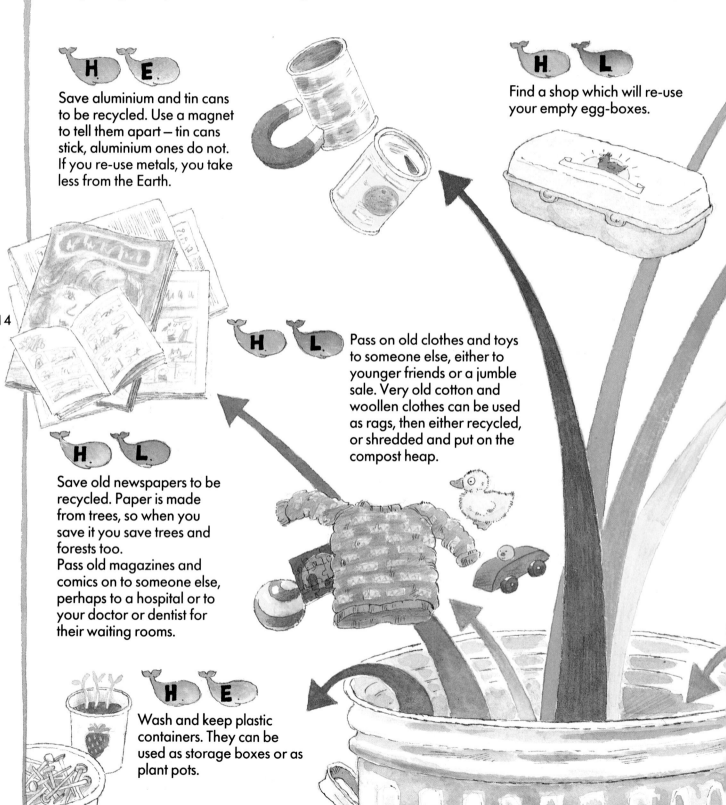

Save glass jars and bottles and take them to the bottle bank.

Put fruit and vegetable peelings on a compost heap. Use your own compost to grow plants instead of buying it.

Save plastic bags to use again for shopping or for lining pedal bins. Most plastic is made from oil, so when you save it you save oil.

What's left in the dustbin?

Not much — only plastic wrappers, crisp packets, waxed cartons, and bones.

What is recycling?

Paper is made from trees. Cans are made from metal. Plastic and acrylic material are made from oil. Every time new things are manufactured they use more of the Earth's resources. But paper and rags can be recycled to make more paper, and cans can be made into new blocks of metal.

15

Do you know?

- Every year a forest the size of Wales is cut down to provide Britain with paper.
- Most families throw away about 40 kg of plastic a year.

Make your own bottle bank, newspaper bin and can collector

Encourage your family to recycle bottles, cans and newspapers by making special boxes to collect them in.

1   Use cardboard boxes large enough and strong enough to hold about 12 bottles.

2   Paint or decorate them to show what each is for. You could cover the can collector with can labels and have one for aluminium cans and one for tins.

Make your own compost

Ask your parents to use the grass clippings and all the other garden rubbish to make a compost heap.

1   Collect vegetable peelings and fruit scraps and add them to the compost heap.

2   As they rot, they form compost. Leave it for about six months until it breaks down into a rich soil.

Make your own plant pots

1 Collect plastic containers.

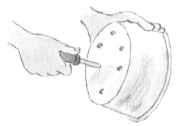

2 Ask an adult to help you make holes in the bottom with an old screwdriver or sharp point.

3 Fill the pots with compost; then plant cuttings or seeds and water them well.

Grow your own beanshoots

Save money and resources by growing your own fast food. You won't need fertilizers or even soil, but you can use your own compost if you like.

2 Sprinkle mung beans over it.

3 Make sure the soil or paper does not dry out. After a few days the seeds will begin to grow into beanshoots.

1 Line the bottom of a shallow tray with a thin layer of damp compost or a damp sheet of kitchen roll (made from recycled paper of course!).

4 They are ready to eat when the leaves open out. They are delicious in salads and sandwiches.

Going shopping

What you buy can help or harm the environment. When you buy things made of, or packaged in, recycled paper, you are helping to save trees.
When you refuse to buy aerosols containing CFCs, you are helping to save the ozone layer.
The Friendly Whale shows you some things to look for when you go shopping.

Sea salt, which is made from seawater and saves rock salt from being mined.

Organic food, which can be healthier for you and the environment.

Biodegradable washing powder, washing-up liquid and other cleaners.

Do you know?

• British companies spend five thousand million pounds a year on packaging

• Not all products which say they are environmentally friendly really are. Read the labels carefully. Mum or Dad can help you to decide.

18

Kitchen roll and toilet rolls made from recycled paper.

Shampoos and hair conditioners which use natural herbs rather than chemicals, and which have not been tested on animals.

Take your own carrier bags with you. Better still, use strong bags and shopping baskets which will last for several years.

Packaging keeps things clean, but don't buy things with too much packaging.

Ask your parents not to buy disposable nappies, particularly those which have been bleached with chlorine. They harm the environment when they are made and when they are thrown away.

If possible buy soft drinks in glass bottles which can be returned or cans which can be recycled.

I've always said looks aren't everything!

What is organic farming?

Organic farmers use only compost and natural manures to help their plants grow. They do not use chemical fertilizers, and so they save the energy and raw materials needed to make fertilizers. Chemicals from fertilizers can harm the environment when they drain into our rivers and lakes. Organic fruit and vegetables may taste better but they do not always look perfect. Organic farmers do not use chemicals to kill pests and fungi which sometimes attack crops.

In the garden

Do you share your garden with lots of other animals or do you keep it just for yourself? If you put pesticides and other chemicals on your plants they may kill pests, but they can also kill birds and helpful insects.

The Friendly Whale shows how your family can encourage birds, butterflies and ladybirds to come into your garden. They will feed on the greenfly and other pests.

Use biodegradable pesticides, but only when necessary. Remember that pesticides are poisonous, so only adults should use them.

If you have a cat which catches birds, a collar with a little bell will help to warn them.

Bats eat thousands of insects every night, so encourage them to come to your garden by putting up a bat box.

Bushes or trees with berries will attract birds, giving them food to eat and places to nest.

If you have room, make a pond in your garden (see page 22). It will provide a refuge for many water creatures and perhaps frogs and water birds. A water butt, or even an old bowl filled with water, will help too. This is the best thing you can do to make your garden wildlife-friendly.

Plant lots of sweet-smelling flowers. They will attract butterflies and moths.

Use your own compost instead of peat and chemical fertilizers.

Put holly leaves around strawberry plants and lettuces to keep the slugs away from them.

Do you know?

• Ladybirds and lacewings are the gardener's friends. Each one will eat thousands of greenfly.
• A well-established city garden may give refuge to 30 kinds of birds, 12 kinds of butterflies, 6 kinds of wild mammals — and you!

Insects and birds love plants

• Butterflies like marigolds, buddleia, lavender, wallflowers, sweet william, and honeysuckle.
• Hoverflies like marigolds, and the herbs dill and fennel. Hoverfly larvae feed on greenfly.
• Blackbirds and thrushes like cotoneaster. These birds eat slugs and snails.
• Goldfinches like thistles.
• Red admiral caterpillars need to feed on nettles.

In the autumn and winter

Make a bird table high up, away from cats.
Put out food and water for the birds, but never close to bushes where cats can hide.
Put out food for the birds in winter. When everywhere is frozen, put out water too.

Add fallen leaves to the compost heap or spread them over the soil to feed worms and make more soil.

Float a ball on your pond in winter, to keep open a hole in the ice so pond animals get enough oxygen.

Do it yourself

Make a garden pond

1   Ask an adult to help you. Draw out the shape of the pond on the ground and dig a hole at least 60 cm deep. The sides should rise in a series of shallow steps.

2   Clean out any sticks and stones from the hole, and line the bottom with bits of old cloth — carpet is ideal. (Be sure there are no chemicals or oil on the cloth.)

3   You will need a large sheet of reinforced PVC plastic. Wash the sheet and lay it carefully into the hole, along the bottom and up the sides. Cover the bottom with a layer of soil, about 10 cm deep.

4   Put bricks round the edges of the sheet while you fill the pond with water from the tap. The water should come to about 10 cm from the top, as the level will rise when it rains. Cover the edges of the sheet with tufts of grass, flat stones or soil. Leave it for a week.

5   Buy some water plants from a garden centre to put in your pond. You can also collect a bucket of water and mud from a friend's pond. It will contain many of the little plants and animals your pond needs. Keep the pond topped up with water in dry weather and never put goldfish in if you want frogs and newts. Goldfish eat the eggs and tadpoles.

If you cannot make a proper pond, an old sink or plastic bowl sunk in the soil will do instead. Frogs, toads and even newts may lay their eggs in it.

Make a nature reserve

Leave part of your garden to grow wild. Plant wildflower mixtures and let dandelions, thistles, buttercups and even nettles, brambles and other weeds grow there. Insects, birds and small mammals such as voles will love it.

Leave part of the lawn uncut until late summer when the seeds of the wild flowers will have formed.

Make a simple bird table

You will need an old tray and two pieces of nylon cord, each about two foot long.

1 Ask an adult to punch a hole at each corner of the tray, plus six more holes all around the tray for rainwater to drain out of.

2 Take one of the pieces of cord and thread it through one of the corner holes. Tie a big knot to fix it. Do the same with the second piece of cord at the other end of the tray.

3 Ask an adult to help you hang your tray on a branch or post — high enough to be out of the reach of cats, but low enough for you to reach.

Things to put on your bird table

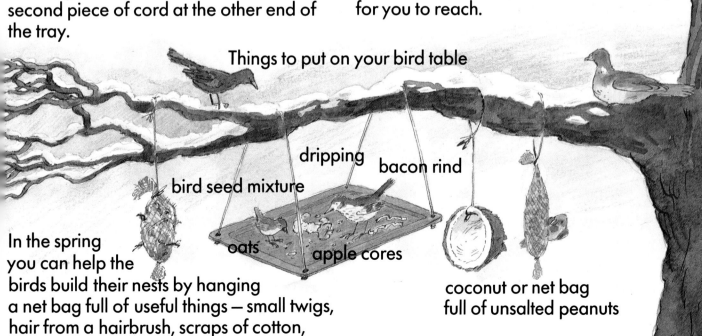

dripping

bird seed mixture

bacon rind

oats

apple cores

In the spring you can help the birds build their nests by hanging a net bag full of useful things — small twigs, hair from a hairbrush, scraps of cotton, string and bits of wool.

coconut or net bag full of unsalted peanuts

How green is your home?

Whales keep themselves warm with their thick layer of blubber, but we use vast amounts of energy to heat our homes. The Friendly Whale shows how you can save some of this energy.

Go round your house with your mum or dad and check how many of these things your house has. Copy or trace the picture of the sun and draw in a ray for every point you score.

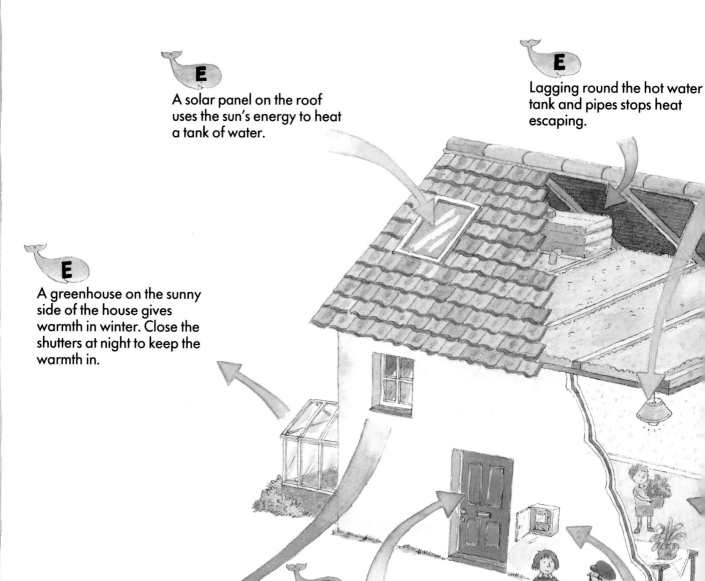

E A solar panel on the roof uses the sun's energy to heat a tank of water.

E Lagging round the hot water tank and pipes stops heat escaping.

E A greenhouse on the sunny side of the house gives warmth in winter. Close the shutters at night to keep the warmth in.

E Two layers of glass on the windows keep heat in. This is called double glazing. Three layers are even better.

E Draught-proofing round doors and windows stops heat leaking out and cold air coming in. This is most important of all.

The next time the electricity and gas meters are read, ask how to read them. The next time oil is delivered, ask how to read the guage. Then you can really see how much energy your house is using.

What is the greenhouse effect?

Whenever we burn coal, petrol, oil or gas it makes a gas called carbon dioxide. Carbon dioxide collects in the air and acts like a blanket around the Earth, keeping it warmer.

Scientists say that if the Earth warms up too much, more places will become deserts and the polar ice caps could start to melt. Then the sea will flood over low land near the coast. We can help to stop this happening by burning less fuel and so saving energy.

25

 E

Longlife light-bulbs last longer and save energy. But be careful. Some people's eyes are sensitive to the fluorescent light.

 E

A thick layer of insulation material on the inside of your roof stops heat leaking out.

E

If the central heating is serviced every year it will work better and use less energy.

 A

Lots of house plants help to clean the air.

 E

Double walls with a space between them can be filled with special material to stop heat leaking through them.

Do you know?

- More than one third of Britain's energy is used by people in their homes.
- About one fifth of energy used at home can be saved by good insulation.
- New houses can be specially designed so that they use only a quarter of the amount of energy used in older houses.

How green is your transport?

Whales travel thousands of kilometres every year using only their muscles. When we walk or cycle we too are using only muscle-power. But when we go by car, bus, train or plane, we are burning oil and pumping waste fumes and carbon dioxide into the air. The Friendly Whale shows how you and your family can make your transport greener and your car cleaner.

If it's too far to walk, try to go by bus or train, not car.

Riding a bicycle is quick and cheap and does not cause pollution.

Leave the car at home and walk whenever you can, especially to and from school.

This car has a lean-burn engine. It uses less fuel than other cars, and makes less harmful fumes.

26

Copy the drawing of the pine tree.
Colour in one of the pine cones for each of the ways you and your family make your transport greener.

What is acid rain?

Gases from exhaust fumes and smoke from power stations and factories are making the clouds slightly acid. Clouds travel — often hundreds of kilometres — before they drop their load of rain, which can be acid enough to damage trees, crops, lakes and rivers.

This garage does not pour used oil down the drains but sends it for recycling.

This family plan their shopping so they only need to take the car to the supermarket once a week.

This car uses unleaded petrol and its exhaust has been modified to cut out most of the harmful fumes.

Use lead-free petrol and help to keep the air cleaner. Too much lead can poison plants, animals and even people.

These children have to go to school by car, but they are sharing it with other classmates.

Do you know?

- Most car journeys in England are less than 3 kilometres long — about half an hour's walk.
- Most cars travel with only one or two people in them.
- One bus can carry as many people as 40 cars usually do.
- 4 out of every 5 trees in Germany's huge Black Forest have been damaged by acid rain.

How green is your neighbourhood?

You can only collect glass bottles, newspaper and cans if there is somewhere to take them to be recycled. We can help to keep waste water clean, but factories must help too.

How many of the things on this page does your local neighbourhood have? Count the green points to see, and write to your local council if you think they can do more for your environment.

A E
• Local shops within walking distance.

H L
• Trees absorb noise and fumes and, while they grow, they lock up carbon dioxide.

A E
• Bus lanes help buses to avoid traffic jams.

H A E
Bicycle lanes make cycling safer.

H L
• Recycling centre for glass, paper, rags and cans.

L
• Road humps make traffic drive more slowly, which is safer for pedestrians.

W A

● Factories can be made to clean up their waste water and waste gases. Visit them on open days and see how they are doing.

L

● Pedestrian crossings make walking safer.

H L

● Wasteground can be made into playgrounds or nature reserves for birds, insects, small mammals and people.

Not the end but a new start for life

The Friendly Whale says she's done her best to show you what to do – now it's up to you. She knows you have a lot of good ideas of your own.

If we can succeed in making the Earth a greener place to live in, then we will not only be helping the whales but all the other plants and animals which share our environment.

Go on, you can do it – and there are plenty of people to give you a helping hand. How about you and your family joining one or more of these organizations?

For you

Watch
The Green
Witham Park
Lincoln LN5 7JR
A nationwide club with many local branches and lots of local and national projects. Membership gives you the right to visit their reserves and learn from the local experts. By the way, I am proud to be their President.

YOC The Young Ornithologists Club
The Lodge
Sandy, Bedfordshire SG19 2DL
Lots of local branches and lots of activity. Join them and learn all about birds, and help to save birds and their habitat.

Wildfowl and Wetlands Trust
Slimbridge
Gloucestershire GL2 7BT
If, like me, you enjoy getting your feet wet, this is the one for you. There are wildfowl parks all round the country where you can meet ducks and geese and swans beak to beak.

Young People's Trust for the Environment and Nature Conservation
95 Woodbridge Road
Guildford
Surrey GU1 4PY
Many schools groups, summer camps and contacts with schools in other countries.

BNA British Naturalists Association
48 Russell Way
Higham Ferrers
Northants NN9 8EJ
Local and school groups, projects and competitions. Learn about natural history with the experts.

Wildflower Society
68 Outwards Road
Loughborough
Leics LE11 3LY
Annual competitions for filling in a diary where you can record every wild flower you see. Help in identification.

To join as you get older

BTCV British Trust for Conservation Volunteers
36 St Mary's Street
Wallingford
Oxfordshire OX10 0EU
They are working all the time to keep our countryside in working order.

Friends of the Earth
26–28 Underwood Street
London N1 7JQ
and

Greenpeace
30–31 Islington Green
London N1 8XE
The two great groups who always speak out for the whales and other wildlife and against pollution and destruction of our environment. With them working for us, our world is a safer place.

For the family

RSPB Royal Society for the Protection of Birds
The Lodge
Sandy
Bedfordshire SG19 2DL
If you are interested in birds and their conservation.

RSNC Royal Society for Nature Conservation
The Green
Witham Park
Lincoln LN5 7JR
The County Wildlife Trusts conservation (lots of work to do and things to learn) in your locality.

Bat Groups of Britain

10 Bedford Cottages
Great Brington
Northampton NN7 4JE
Through them you can find out about bats and learn how to make a bat box for your garden.

Woodland Trust

Autumn Park
Dysart Road
Grantham
Lincolnshire NG31 600
They get local people to club together and buy and manage local woodland.

National Trust

36 Queen Anne's Gate
London SW1H 9AS
A ticket for the whole family to visit some of our best countryside estates and best stretches of coastline.

WWF World Wide Fund for Nature

Panda House
Wayside Park
Catteshall Lane
Godalming
Surrey GU7 1XR
With their PANDA logo and their expertise for wildlife conservation, they are the top of the conservational pops.

Work with us to save the world.
Thank you for caring.

David Bellamy

PS The Friendly Whale says thank you, too.

Index

ALSO BY DAVID BELLAMY:
THE **OUR CHANGING WORLD** SERIES

The Roadside

An exploration of the environment of the roadside, and what happens
when people threaten to obliterate a farm track by
building a six-lane motorway in its place.

ISBN 0-7112-1383-6   £4.99

The Rockpool

A tale of the fascinating animal and plant life in the ever-changing world
of the rockpool, and the way it is affected by a disastrous oil spill.

ISBN 0-7112-1386-0   £4.99

The River

A story of the birds, fish and plants that live in and on the banks of the river,
and how they are affected by pollution from a nearby factory.

ISBN 0-7112-1387-9   £4.99

The Forest

A beautifully-illustrated exploration of the animal and plant life of the forest,
and what happens when an ancient, storm-damaged oak tree is cut down.

ISBN 0-7112-1385-2 £4.99

The *Our Changing World* series is suitable for National Curriculum Science,
Key Stages 1 and 2; English – Reading, Key Stages 1 and 2
Scottish Guidelines Environmental Studies, Levels B and C;
English Language – Reading, Levels B and C

Frances Lincoln titles are available from all good bookshops.
Prices are correct at time of printing, but may be subject to change.